# Pilots

## The Ultimate Collection of Pilot Jokes

By Chester Croker

**Jokes for Pilots**

These jokes for pilots will make you laugh. Some of these jokes are old, some of them are new and we hope you enjoy our collection of the very best pilot jokes and puns around.

These funny pilot jokes are simply guaranteed to make you laugh.

Prepare for take-off.

Published by Glowworm Press
7 Nuffield Way
Abingdon OX14 1RL

# FOREWORD

When I was asked to write a foreword to this book I was deeply flattered.

That is until I was told that I was the last resort by the author, Chester Croker, and that everyone else he had approached had said they couldn't do it!

I have known Chester for a number of years and his ability to create funny jokes is absolutely incredible. He is quick witted and an expert at crafting clever puns and amusing gags and I feel he is the ideal man to put together a joke book about our high flying profession.

He will be glad you have bought this book, as he has an expensive lifestyle to maintain.

Enjoy!

Ted Striker

# Table of Contents

# Chapter 1: Pilot Jokes

If you're looking for some funny pilot jokes you've certainly come to the right place.

We've got some great one-liners to start with, loads of pilot to tower communication funnies, plenty of quick fire questions and answers themed gags, many story led jokes, a number of humorous quotes and as a bonus some cheesy pick-up lines that pilots could try.

This mixture of pilot jokes will prove that pilots have a good sense of humor.

Prepare for take-off, and chocks away!

## Chapter 2: One Liner Pilot Jokes

Two wrongs don't make a right but two Wrights made an airplane.

---

A male pilot is a confused soul who talks about women when he is flying; and about flying when he is with a woman.

---

Confucius says, "Man who runs through airport turnstile, backwards, going Bangkok."

---

To most people, the sky is the limit. To those who love aviation, the sky is home.

---

I got called pretty yesterday and it felt good.

Actually, the full sentence was "You're a pretty bad pilot." but I'm choosing to focus on the positive.

Tower: "You have traffic at 10 o'clock, 6 miles."

Pilot: "Give us another hint - we have digital watches!"

---

The difference between flight attendants and jet engines is that the engine usually quits whining when it gets to the gate.

---

A plane crashed into a cemetery earlier today. Search and rescue workers have recovered 25 bodies so far but expect that number to climb as digging continues.

---

I will always remember being told at pilot training that, "Getting high is part of the job description."

---

Takeoffs are optional. Landings are mandatory.

Did you hear about the student pilot who stole a calendar?  He got twelve months.

---

As we landed in Saudi Arabia the pilot announced, "Ladies and Gentlemen, don't forget to adjust your watches to local time."

I thought to myself, "How do I turn it back to the 14th century?"

---

Did you hear about the cross-eyed pilot who got sacked because he couldn't see eye to eye with his crew.

---

It's better to break ground and head into the wind than to break wind and head into the ground.

A pilot friend of mine gave me some great advice, saying I should put something away for a rainy day. I've gone for an umbrella.

---

Overheard on RyanAir:- "Last one off the plane must clean it."

---

A pilot wanted to buy something nice for his boss, so he bought him a new chair. His boss won't let him plug it in though.

---

If you push the stick forward, the houses get bigger.

If you pull the stick back they get smaller. (unless you keep pulling the stick back -- then they get bigger again)

---

Flying is not dangerous; crashing is dangerous.

Without ammunition the USAF would be just another expensive flying club.

---

Overheard:- I give that landing a "9"……. on the Richter scale.

---

Unknown landing signal officer to US Navy aircraft carrier pilot after his 4th unsuccessful landing attempt: "You've got to land here son, this is where the food is."

---

The probability of survival is equal to the angle of arrival.

A flight attendant's comment on a less than perfect landing:- "We ask you to please remain seated as Captain Kangaroo bounces us to the terminal."

---

Yesterday, a pilot's wife asked him to pass her lipstick but he passed her a super-glue stick instead by mistake. She still isn't talking to him.

---

Those who hoot with the owls by night should not fly with the eagles by day.

---

Overheard: "Thank you for flying Delta Business Express. We hope you enjoyed giving us the business as much as we enjoyed taking you for a ride."

---

Pilot Training:- Try to keep the number of your landings equal to the number of your takeoffs.

## Chapter 3: Pilot Tower Communications

Approach: "United 329 heavy, your traffic is a Fokker, one o'clock, four miles, eastbound."

United 239: "Approach, I've always wanted to say this - I've got the little Fokker in sight."

---

Approach: "Cessna X, your mode C is intermittently reporting 3,000 feet. Say your altitude."

Pilot: "Cessna X is intermittently at 3,000 feet."

---

Tower: "Traffic at your 6 o'clock, 2 miles, same altitude, closing slowly."

Pilot: "Roger. Since our plane doesn't come with rear view mirrors, could you keep us appraised?"

---

Tower: "Cessna 312, Can you give us a pilot report?"

Pilot: "It feels like we're riding a hotel's vibrating bed up here."

Tower: "Is that bed on the light, moderate or rattle your teeth setting?"

---

Pilot: "Tower, we'd like to report a family of foxes that are crossing the taxiway."

Tower: "Roger that. The foxes help keep families of birds from nesting in the area."

---

Tower: "Kilo Mike Delta, are you proceeding to TGO?"

Pilot: "Yes Sir, more or less."

Tower: "In that case, proceed a little bit more to TGO."

---

Approach Control: "747 Heavy, traffic is a 777 at your 2 o'clock at 6000 feet."

747 Heavy: "Roger, Approach, we have that light twin in sight."

---

Ground Control: "Airliner Y, Good news, you are clear to taxi to the active."

Pilot: "Roger. What's the bad news?"

Ground Control: "No bad news at the moment, but you probably want to get going before I find any."

---

Pilot: "O'Hare Tower, Bonanza X, request landing. I can land on any runway and hold short of any other runway."

Tower: "Roger, we request you land at Chicago Executive and hold short of O'Hare."

---

Tower: "Speedbird356, proceed to stand 69."

BA Pilot: "Yes, Sir. Nose in or Nose out?"

---

Pilot: "Tower, could we get an EFC?"

Tower: "Indefinite."

Pilot: "I'm pretty sure we don't have enough fuel for that."

---

ATC: "Piper N4455D, traffic at your 2 o'clock, 500 feet below you."

Piper N4455D: "Well, we see a light coming towards us."

ATC: "Look again - there's probably a plane behind that light."

---

Tower: "Airliner X, it looks like you have a baggage door open."

Pilot: "Thank you for the report, but that must be our APU door that's open for cooling."

Tower: "Airliner X, you have luggage falling out of your APU door."

---

Student Pilot: "Tower, Cessna Z, Requesting help determining my location, I'm lost."

Tower: "Can you fly over any identifiable man-made objects like a highway or water tower?"

Pilot: "Affirmative, I just flew by a water tower, but all it said was "Class of '09."

---

Tower: "Gulfstream X, You're cleared to 9,000 feet. For a vector to Hector, contact the sector director."

---

Controller: "Flight X, can you climb to FL390?"

Pilot: "Standby."

A few seconds pass.

Pilot: "We can make it, but we'll have to throw out a few passengers."

Controller: "That's approved."

---

Pilot: "Condor 471, don't you have a Follow-me?"

Tower: "Negative. Let's just see how your find your own way to Gate 13."

---

Tower: "Delta Zulu Hotel, turn right now and report your heading."

Pilot: "Wilco. 341, 342, 343, 344, 345..."

---

Tower: "Airliner 757 vectored 310 at 145 knots behind traffic."

Pilot: "Roger that, 310 at 145 to clean out the stall horn."

---

Approach: "Airliner Heavy, report your airspeed for spacing."

Pilot: "Approach, we're really hauling ass."

Approach: "Airliner Heavy, I couldn't care less about your cargo, I need to know your airspeed."

---

Pilot: "Request heading 110 to avoid."

Tower: "To avoid what?"

Pilot: "To avoid delay."

---

Tower: "Hotel Papa Zulu, climb four thousand to six thousand and maintain."

Pilot: "Hotel Papa Zulu, climbing flight level 100."

Tower: "Hotel Papa Zulu, climb to flight level 60 and maintain."

Pilot: "But 4 and 6 is 10, isn't it?"

Tower: "You're supposed to climb, not add."

---

Tower: "Delta Fox Alpha, hold position. The marshall will park you."

Pilot: "Roger. We're looking out for John Wayne."

---

Tower: "Cessna 315, that taxiway is approved for single engine use only."

Pilot: "Roger, shutting down one engine."

---

Pilot: "Good morning, Frankfurt ground, KLM 252 request start up and push back, please."

Tower: "KLM 252 expect start up in two hours."

Pilot: "Please confirm: two hours delay?"

Tower: "Affirmative."

Pilot: "In that case, cancel the good morning."

---

Pilot: "Logan Ground, Radio Check."

Tower: "You sound like you are calling from inside a tin can."

Pilot: "Roger. It feels like it, too."

---

Pilot: "Airliner X, request a 360 to parking."

Tower: "360 approved, 180 recommended."

---

Tower: "Eastern 802, cleared for takeoff, contact Departure on 124.7."

Eastern 802: "Tower, Eastern 802 switching to Departure. By the way, after we lifted off we saw some kind of dead animal on the far end of the runway."

Tower: "Continental 735, cleared for takeoff, contact Departure on124.7. Did you copy that report from Eastern?"

Continental 735: "Continental 735, cleared for takeoff, roger; and yes, we copied Eastern and we've already notified our caterers."

---

Tower: "Have you got enough fuel or not?"

Pilot: "Yes."

Tower: "Yes what?"

Pilot: "Yes, Sir!"

---

Pilot: "Tower, please call me a fuel truck."

Tower: "Roger. You are a fuel truck."

---

Tower: "Say fuel state."

Pilot: "Fuel state."

Tower: "Say again."

Pilot: "Again."

Tower: "Argh, give me your fuel!"

Pilot: "Sorry, need it for myself."

---

Tower: "Lufthansa 375, you are number one, check for workers on the taxiway."

Pilot: "Roger. We've checked; they are all working."

---

Controller: "Mission 123, do you have problems?"

Pilot: "I think I have lost my compass."

Controller: "Judging the way you are flying, you've lost the whole instrument panel."

---

Pilot: "Tower, give me a rough time check."

Tower: "It's Thursday."

---

Pilot: "Tower, student pilot, I am out of fuel."

Tower: "Roger that. Reduce airspeed to best glide. Do you have the airfield in sight?"

Pilot: "Uh, Tower. I am on the north ramp. I just want to know where the fuel truck is."

---

Tower: "Hawk 220, is this the same aircraft declaring an emergency about an hour ago?"

Pilot: "Negative, Sir. It's only the same pilot."

---

Pilot: "Tower, there's a runway light burning."

Tower: "I'm sure there are dozens of lights burning."

Pilot: "Sorry, I mean it's smoking."

---

Controller: "United 26, make a 360."

Pilot: "Approach, this here is a 747 that costs $12,000 per hour to operate. A 360 takes 10 minutes."

Controller: "Great, give me a $2,000 turn."

---

Tower: "What's your height and position?"

Pilot: "I'm 6 foot 3 inches tall and I'm sitting front left."

---

Tower: "TWA 2841, for noise abatement turn right 45 Degrees."

TWA 2841: "Center, we are at 35,000 feet. How much noise can we make up here?"

Tower: "Sir, have you ever heard the noise a 747 makes when it hits a 737?"

---

Tower: "Cannot read you; say again."

Pilot: "Again."

---

ATC: "N123XY, say altitude."

N123XY: "Altitude."

ATC: "N123XY, say airspeed."

N123XY: "Airspeed."

ATC: "N123XY, say cancel IFR."

N123XY: "Eight thousand feet, one hundred fifty knots indicated."

---

United cargo jet (with female pilot): "This is my secondary radio. Is my transmission still fuzzy?"

ARTCC controller: "I don't know. I've never seen it."

---

Unknown aircraft: "I'm #*&$ bored."

Air Traffic Control: "Last aircraft transmitting, identify yourself immediately."

Unknown aircraft: "I said I was #*&$ bored, not #&*$ stupid."

---

A DC-10 had an extremely long rollout after landing with his approach speed a little high.

San Jose Tower: "American 753 heavy, turn right at the end of the runway, if able. If not able, take the Guadalupe exit off Highway 101 and make a right at the light to return to the airport."

---

An airliner was in a holding pattern waiting for the Democratic Presidential Nominee to leave the area.

Tower: "Airliner X, can you hold for another 10 minutes?"

Pilot: "Yes sir, however, please advise the Democrats that more and more passengers are turning Republican."

---

Tower: "Can you give me your position?"

Pilot: "I'm next to a cloud that looks like an elephant."

Tower: "Can you me more specific?"

Pilot: "It looks like Dumbo."

---

It was a really nice day, right about dusk, and a Piper Malibu was being vectored into a long line of airliners in order to land at Kansas City.

KC Approach: "Malibu three-two Charlie, you're following a 727, one o'clock and three miles."

Three-two Charlie: "We've got him. We'll follow him."

KC Approach: "Delta 105, your traffic to follow is a Malibu, eleven o'clock and three miles. Do you have that traffic?"

Delta 105 (in a thick southern drawl): "Well, I've got something down there. I can't quite tell if it's a Malibu or a Chevelle."

---

Kids on a tour of the Tower: "Have you ever had a real emergency?"

Controller: "There was that one time when we ran out of coffee."

---

The German air traffic controllers at Frankfurt Airport can be a short-tempered lot. They not only expect one to know one's gate parking location but also how to get there without any assistance from them.

So it was with some amusement that we listened to the following exchange between Frankfurt ground control and a British Airways plane (call sign "Speedbird 206") after landing:

Speedbird 206: "Top of the morning Frankfurt, Speedbird 206 clear of the active runway."

Ground: "Guten morgen. You will taxi to your gate."

The big British Airways plane pulled onto the main taxiway and slowed to a stop.

Ground: "Speedbird 206, do you not know where you are going?"

Speedbird 206: "Stand by a moment ground, I'm looking up our gate location now."

Ground (with some arrogant impatience): "Speedbird 206, you have never flown to Frankfurt before?"

Speedbird 206 (coolly): "Yes, I have, in 1944. In another type of plane, at night, but I didn't stop."

---

# Chapter 4: Question and Answer Pilot Jokes

Q: How does the captain know the aircraft is safely at the ramp?

A: *Both the engines and the co-pilot stop whining.*

---

Q: What do you call a space pilot who lives dangerously?

A: *Han YOLO.*

---

Q: A plane crashed and every single person died except two, why?

A: *Because they were a couple.*

---

Q: What's the difference between a fighter pilot and God?

A: *God doesn't think He's a fighter pilot.*

---

Q: What do you get when you cross an airplane with a magician?

A: A *flying sorcerer.*

Q: What is it called when you're sick of being in an airport?

A: *Terminal illness.*

---

Q: Why do 747s have humps?

A: *So the pilot can sit on his wallet.*

---

Q: Want to know how to make a small fortune running a charter airline?

A: *Start out with a large one.*

---

Q: What do you call a pregnant flight attendant?

A: *Pilot error.*

---

Q: Why can't spiders become pilots?

A: *Because they only know how to tailspin.*

Q: What kind of chocolate do they sell at the airport?

A: *Plane Chocolate.*

---

Q: What do you call a plane that's about to crash?

A: *An "Error Plane."*

---

Q: Why don`t ducks tell jokes when they fly?

A: *Because they would quack up!*

---

Q: What do you a call pilot that took economics?

A: *Anna F.*

---

Q: Why did the cannibal pilot get disciplined by his bosses?

A: *For buttering up his crew.*

Q: Where can you find Tom Cruise on a flight?

A: *In Risky Business class.*

---

Q: What do you call a flying primate?

A: *A hot air baboon.*

---

Q: How do you know you're flying over Bulgaria?

A: *There is toilet paper hanging on the clothes lines.*

---

Q: What do you call an old pilot who is happy every Monday?

A: *Retired.*

## Chapter 5: Short Pilot Jokes

I saw a police officer wearing a pilot's uniform yesterday.

I thought it was a bit odd.

Then I realized he was one of those plane clothes cops.

---

A man telephoned an airline office in New York and asked, "How long does it take to fly to Boston?"

The clerk said, "Just a minute."

"Thank you," the man said and hung up.

---

It was mealtime on a small airline and the flight attendant asked a passenger if he would like dinner.

"What are my choices?" he asked.

"Yes or No," she replied.

---

A dog walks into a pub, and sits down. He says to the barman, "Can I have a pint of lager and a packet of peanuts please."

The barman, who has never seen a talking dog before, says, "Wow, that's incredible - you should join the circus!'"

The talking dog replies, "Why? What do they need pilots for?"

---

A 747 was having engine trouble, and the pilot instructed the cabin crew to get the passengers to take their seats and get prepared for an emergency landing.

A few minutes later, the pilot asked the flight attendants if everyone was buckled in and ready.

"We're all set back here, Captain," came the reply, "except the lawyers are still going around handing out business cards."

---

A 65 years old pilot was walking in the park one day when he came across a frog.

He reached down, picked the frog up, and started to put it in his pocket. As he did so, the frog said, "Kiss me on the lips and I'll turn into a beautiful woman and show you a very good time."

The old pilot continued to put the frog in his pocket.

The frog croaked, "Didn't you hear what I said?"

The pilot looked at the frog and said, "Yes, but at my age I'd rather have a talking frog."

---

The propeller is just a big fan at the front of the plane to keep the pilot cool.

Want proof?

Simply make it stop; then watch the pilot break out into a sweat.

---

A blonde gets to fly in an airplane for the first time. She was very excited and as soon as she boarded the plane, a Boeing 747, she started jumping up and down in excitement, shouting, "BOEING! BOEING! BOEING!"

The pilot was so annoyed by the goings on, he comes out of the flight deck and tells her, "Be silent."

She stared at the pilot for a moment, concentrated really hard, and then started shouting, "OEING! OEING! OEING!

---

Every one already knows the definition of a "good landing" is one from which you can walk away.

But very few know the definition of a "great landing."

It's one after which you can use the airplane another time.

---

One day in the not too distant future, so they say, airliners will have only two crew members on the flight deck - a pilot and a dog.

At the press conference on the occasion of the introduction of the first of those airliners, a journalists asks, "What is the job of the dog?"

The PR person replies, "To bite the pilot if he touches the controls."

The journalist replies, "That makes sense. But why keep the pilot in the cockpit?"

The PR person answers, "Someone has to feed the dog!"

---

A senior stewardess told her younger colleague, "I like to keep in shape, so I go the gym and do pilots."

The younger stewardess said, "Don't you mean Pilates?"

The older stewardess replied, "I know what I mean, honey."

---

A mother and her young son were flying Aloha Airlines from Honolulu to Los Angeles.

The boy asked the stewardess, "If big dogs have baby dogs and big cats have baby cats, why don't big planes have baby planes?"

The stewardess responded, "Did your mother tell you to ask me?"

The boy replied, "Yes."

The stewardess responded, "Tell your mother that there are no baby planes because Aloha always pulls out on time. Your mother can explain it to you."

---

A student became lost during a solo cross-country flight.

While attempting to locate the aircraft on radar, ATC asked, "What was your last known position?"

The student replied, "When I was number one for take-off."

A pilot took his cross-eyed cat to the vet.

The vet picked the cat up to examine her and said, "Sorry, I'm going to have to put her down."

The pilot said, "It's not that bad is it?"

The vet replied, "No, she's just very heavy."

---

A female pilot at Sydney's Bankstown airport was in a hurry to get airborne, and she made the following request, "Bankstown Tower Cessna ABC requests an intersexual departure runway 29R."

Almost straight away ATC replied, "ABC, The full length is available."

---

What is the similarity between air traffic controllers and pilots?

If a pilot screws up, the pilot dies.

If ATC screws up, the pilot dies.

---

A pilot complained to his friend that his wife didn't satisfy him anymore.

His friend advised he find another woman on the side, pretty sharpish.

When they met up a month or so later, the pilot told his friend, "I took your advice. I actually managed to find two women on the side, yet my wife still doesn't satisfy me."

---

After take-off, the pilot thought he'd play the digital tape recorder, as he had a very sore throat.

In the cabin, the passengers heard the soothing, reassuring voice of the pilot, "Ladies and gentlemen, this is your automatic pilot. In this modern and carefully tested system any error is absolutely impossible, absolutely impossible, absolutely impossible..."

---

Taxiing down the tarmac, the jetliner abruptly stopped, turned around and returned to the gate.

After an hour-long wait, it finally took off.

A concerned passenger asked the flight attendant, "What was the problem?"

"The pilot was bothered by a noise he heard in the engine," explained the flight attendant, "and it took us a while to find a new pilot."

---

A pilot goes to see his doctor about a hearing problem he is having.

The doctor says, "Can you describe the symptoms to me?"

The pilot replies, "Yes. Homer is a fat yellow lazy man and his wife Marge is skinny with big blue hair."

---

After take-off a pilot accidentally left his microphone on and said to his co-pilot, "Now I just want a cup of coffee and a blowjob."

An air hostess ran down the aisle to tell him to switch off his microphone.

As she ran past, one of the passengers shouted, "Don't forget the coffee."

---

A man walks up to the customer services counter at the airport.

"Can I help you?" asks the agent.

"I want a round trip ticket," says the man.

"Where to?" asks the agent.

The man replies, "Back to here."

---

A pilot is late for duty and is struggling to find a parking space.

"Lord," he prayed. "I just can't cope with this. If you open a space up for me, I swear I'll give up the booze and go to church every Sunday."

Suddenly, the clouds part and the sun shines onto an empty parking spot.

Without missing a beat, the pilot says, "Never mind Lord, I found one."

---

At McCarran airport, I told the lady at the United check-in desk, "Send one of my bags to New York, send one to Los Angeles, and send one to Miami."

She said, "We can't do that."

I told her, "You did last week."

---

A young newly qualified pilot is sitting at a bar one night, when a big construction worker sits down next to him.

They start talking and eventually the conversation gets on to nuclear war.

The pilot asks the construction worker, "If you were to hear the early warning sirens go off and you know you only have twenty minutes left to live, what would you do?"

The construction worker replies, "I am going to get it on with anything that moves."

The construction worker then asks the young pilot what he would do to which he replies, "I am going to keep perfectly still."

---

As we waited just off the runway for another airliner to cross in front of us, some of the passengers were beginning to retrieve luggage from the overhead bins.

The first officer announced on the intercom, "This aircraft is equipped with a video surveillance system that monitors the cabin during taxiing. Any passengers not remaining in their seats until the aircraft comes to a full and complete stop at the gate will be strip-searched as they leave the aircraft."

---

A proud father is showing pictures of his three sons to an old friend when he is asked, "What do your boys do for a living?"

He replied, "Well my youngest is a neurosurgeon and my middle is a lawyer."

"What does the oldest child do?" his friend asked.

The reply came, "He's the pilot that paid for the others' education."

---

A pilot meets up with his blonde girlfriend as she's picking up her car from the mechanic.

"Everything ok with your car now?" he asks.

"Yes, thank goodness," the dipsy blonde replies.

He says, "Weren't you concerned the mechanic might try to rip you off?"

She replies, "Yes, but he didn't. I was so relieved when he told me that all I needed was blinker fluid!"

---

The airline had a policy which required the First Officer to stand at the door while the passengers exited, smile, and say, "Thanks for flying our Airline."

One time after a particularly bad landing, a little old lady asked the First Officer, "Sir, do you mind if I ask you a question?"

"Why, no, Ma'am," he replied. "What is it?"

The little old lady said, "Did we land, or were we shot down?"

---

After a real crusher of a landing in Phoenix, the flight attendant came on the PA and said, "Ladies and Gentlemen, please remain in your seats until Captain Crash and the crew have brought the aircraft to a screeching halt against the gate. Once the tire smoke has cleared and the warning bells are silenced, we'll open the door and you can pick your way through the wreckage to the terminal."

---

A witty pilot comes on the intercom and says, "Folks, we have reached our cruising altitude now, so I am going to switch the seat belt sign off."

He continues, "Feel free to move about as you wish, but please stay inside the plane till we land. It's a bit cold outside, and if you walk on the wings it affects the flight pattern."

---

A pilot tries to enter a smart cocktail bar wearing a shirt open at the collar, but the doorman turns him away saying that he needs to wear a necktie to gain entry.

So the pilot goes to his car and in desperation he ties some jump leads around his neck, and somehow manages to create a knot and he lets the cable ends dangle free.

He goes back to the bar and the doorman carefully looks him over, and says, "OK, I guess you can come in - just don't start anything."

---

After a very hard landing in Salt Lake City, a flight attendant came on the intercom and said, "That was quite a bump and I know what y'all are thinking. I'm here to tell you it wasn't the airline's fault, it wasn't the pilot's fault, it wasn't the flight attendant's fault; it was the asphalt."

On an American Airlines flight into Amarillo, Texas, on a particularly windy and bumpy day, the Captain was really having to fight it during the final approach.

After an extremely hard landing, the Flight Attendant came on the PA and announced, "Ladies and Gentlemen, welcome to Amarillo. Please remain in your seats with your seat belts fastened while the Captain taxis what's left of our airplane to the gate."

---

Overheard on Norwegian:- "As you exit the plane, please make sure to gather all of your belongings. Anything left behind will be distributed evenly among the flight attendants. Please do not leave children or spouses."

---

While waiting for start clearance in Munich I overheard the following:-

Lufthansa (in German): "Ground, what is our start clearance time?"

Ground (in English): "If you want an answer you must speak English."

Lufthansa (in English): "I am a German, flying a German airplane, in Germany. Why must I speak English?"

Unknown voice (in a beautiful British accent): "Because you lost the bloody war!"

# Chapter 6: Memorable Aviation Quotes

Keep the aeroplane in such an attitude that the air pressure is directly in the pilot's face. - *Horatio C. Barber, 1916*

---

The only time an aircraft has too much fuel on board is when it is on fire. - *Sir Charles Kingsford Smith, 1920's*

---

Just remember, if you crash because of weather your funeral will be held on a sunny day. - *Layton A. Bennett*

---

I hope you either take up parachute jumping or stay out of single-motored airplanes at night. - *Charles A. Lindbergh, to Wiley Post, 1931*

---

If you want to grow old as a pilot, you've got to know when to push it, and when to back off. – *Chuck Yeager*

---

Keep thy airspeed up, less the earth come from below and smite thee. - *William Kershner*

---

Instrument flying is when your mind gets a grip on the fact that there is vision beyond sight. - *U.S. Navy 'Approach' magazine 1940's.*

---

Never fly in the same cockpit with someone braver than you. - *Richard Herman Jr., 'Firebreak'*

---

There is no reason to fly through a thunderstorm in peacetime. - *Sign over squadron ops desk at Davis-Monthan AFB, 1970's*

---

The engine is the heart of an airplane, but the pilot is its soul. – *Walter Alexander Raleigh*

---

*If you have a quote you would like to see included in the next version of this book, please visit the glowwormpress.com website.*

---

## Chapter 7: Longer Pilot Jokes

### A Classic Piece of Navigation

A pilot was flying a small single engine charter plane, with a couple of very important executives on board. He was coming into Seattle airport through thick fog with less than 10m visibility when his instruments went out. So he began circling around looking for a landmark. After half an hour or so, he starts running pretty low on fuel and the passengers are getting nervous.

Finally, a small opening in the fog appears and he sees a tall building with a window open. The pilot banks the plane around, rolls down the window and shouts to the guy, "Hey. Where am I?" The office worker replies, "You're in a plane."

The pilot rolls up the window, executes a 275 degree turn and proceeds to execute a perfect blind landing on the runway of the airport 5 miles away. Just as the plane stops, so does the engine as the fuel has run out.

The passengers are amazed and one asks the pilot how he managed to land the plane safely.

"Simple," replies the pilot, "I asked the guy in that building a simple question. The answer he gave me was 100 per cent correct but absolutely useless, therefore I knew that must be Microsoft's support office building and from there I knew the airport was just 5 miles away."

## Blonde Stewardess

An airline captain was breaking in a new blonde stewardess. The route they were flying had a layover in another city.

Upon their arrival, the captain showed the stewardess the best places for airline personnel to eat, shop and stay overnight.

The next morning, as the pilot was preparing the crew for the day's route, he noticed the new stewardess was missing.

He knew which room she was in at the hotel and called her up wondering what happened.

She answered the phone, crying, and said she couldn't get out of her room.

"You can't get out of your room?" the captain asked, "Why not?"

The stewardess replied, "There are only three doors in here," she sobbed, "one is the bathroom, one is the closet, and one has a sign on it that says 'Do Not Disturb.'"

# The Old Man

A guy is in a store when he sees an old man crying his eyes out, so he asks him what's the matter.

"I've had a great life," says the old man. "I ran a successful pilot training school, and I sold my company for loads of money."

The guy says, "So what's the problem?"

The old man says, "I built myself a large house with a swimming pool."

The guy looks puzzled and says, "Okay, so what's the problem?"

The old man sobs, "I own a beautiful car."

The guy scratches his head and says, "I still don't see what the problem is."

The old man says, "Last month I got married to a 25 year old Playboy bunny."

The guy loses his temper. "Come on, old timer, what is the problem?"

The old man wails, "I can't remember where I live!"

# Intercom

An Airbus 380 was coming into London Heathrow after a long-haul trip from Singapore and the captain opened the intercom and said 'Ladies and gentlemen we are now making our final approach into Heathrow, we hope you've enjoyed flying with Singapore Airlines and that we'll see you again soon, please have a safe onward journey' at which point he forgot to turn the intercom off.

He turned to the co-pilot and said "Well Mike, what plans do you have for the rest of the day?"

The co-pilot replied, "My wife will be at the hotel and she's got seats booked for a West-End show. What plans do you have?"

The captain said, "As you know my divorce was finalised last week so I'll be taking a long soak in the bath before ordering dinner in my room. I'm thinking that after that I'll call the pretty new blonde stewardess working upstairs, Susanne I think her name is, and take her out for a drink then take her back to my room and give her a damn good seeing to."

At that moment the passengers cheered loudly and in the upper deck Susanne realised the intercom was still on by accident and she had to get downstairs and let them know.

She ran down the aisle and tripped headlong over an old lady's handbag which was poking out into the aisle.

The old lady looked down at the spread-eagled young woman and said, "There's no need to hurry love, he's going to have a bath first."

# Flying in the 'Old Days'

In the early 1930's, a farmer and his wife went to a fair. The farmer was fascinated by the airplanes and asked a pilot how much a ride would cost.

"$10 for 3 minutes," replied the pilot.

"That's too much," said the farmer.

The pilot thought for a second and then said, "I'll make you a deal. If you and your wife ride for 3 minutes without uttering a sound, the ride will be free. But if you make a sound, you'll have to pay $10."

The farmer and his wife agreed and went for a wild ride. After they landed, the pilot said to the farmer, "I want to congratulate you for not making a sound. You are a brave man."

"Maybe so," said the farmer, "But I got to tell ya, I almost screamed when my wife fell out."

## Three Pilots

There was a Mexican, an American and a Japanese pilot taking turns flying over each of their countries. They were flying over Japan and the Japanese guy drops an apple on his country and the other two ask why he did that and he said, "Because I love my country."

They went onto Mexico and the Mexican drops an orange on his country so the other two asked why he did that and he said, "Because I love my country."

They went on to America and the American drops a bomb on his country so the other two asked him why he did that and he said, "Because I hate my country."

Later, they landed in their respective countries.

The Japanese guy saw a kid crying so he asked what happened and the kid said an apple fell out of the sky and hit him in the head.

The Mexican saw a kid crying so he asked what happened and the kid said an orange fell out of the sky and hit him in the head.

The American saw a kid laughing so he asked what happened and the kid said, "I farted and the building behind me exploded."

## Engine Failure

Two Irish guys are flying from Belfast to New York. They take off, and after a while, the pilot comes on the PA and informs the passengers that they have lost one of the engines quit but not to worry, the other three are still OK but the flight will take a bit longer.

Half an hour later, the pilot comes on the PA system again and says they just lost another engine, but no worries, they'll continue on but the flight will take a bit longer.

Half an hour later, the pilot comes back on the PA and says they have just lost number 3.

One Irish guy says to the other, "Christ, if we lose that last engine we'll be up here all day."

## Three Friends

Ron is talking to two of his friends, Jim and Shamus.

Jim says, "I think my wife is having an affair with a pilot. The other day I came home and found a flight case under our bed."

Shamus then confides, "Crikey, me too. I think my wife is having an affair with an electrician. The other day I found wire cutters under our bed."

Ron thinks for a minute and then says, "You know - I think my wife is having an affair with a horse."

Both Jim and Shamus look at him suspiciously.

Ron sees them looking at him and says, "No, seriously. The other day I came home early and found a jockey under our bed."

## The Irate Controller

While taxi-ing at Miami, the crew of a Delta Airbus departing for Atlanta made a wrong turn and came nose to nose with an American 767.

The irate female ground controller lashed out at the Delta air crew, screaming, "Delta 891, where are you going? I told you to turn right onto Charlie taxiway. You turned right on Bravo. Stop right there. I know it's difficult for you to tell the difference between B's and C's, but you need to get it right."

Continuing her rant to the embarrassed crew, she was now shouting hysterically, "You've screwed everything up. It'll take me ages to sort this out. You stay right there and don't move till I tell you to. You can expect progressive taxi instructions in about half an hour and I want you to go exactly where I tell you, when I tell you, and how I tell you. You got that, Delta 891?"

"Yes ma'am," the chastened crew responded.

Unsurprisingly the ground control frequency went silent after the verbal bashing of Delta 891.

Nobody wanted to engage the irate ground controller in her current state. Tension in every cockpit at MIA was running high when an unknown pilot broke the silence and softly asked, "Wasn't I married to you once?"

## Dumb Passenger

A beautiful young blonde woman boards a plane to Dallas with a ticket in economy class. Noticing an empty seat in first class, she moves to the front and sits down.

The flight attendant checks her ticket and tells the woman she needs to move back to economy. The blonde replies, "I don't think so. I'm going to sit here until we get to Dallas."

The captain, having been informed of the situation, goes back and tells the blonde that her assigned seat is in economy, and again, she replies the same.

Not wanting to cause a commotion, the captain returns to the cockpit to discuss the situation with the first officer. The FO says that his girlfriend is blonde, and that he will take care of it. He goes back and whispers something in the blonde's ear.

Immediately she gets up, thanks the FO, and returns to economy.

The captain and flight attendant are stunned and ask the FO how he was able to so quickly diffuse the situation.

The FO replies, "I just told her that the first class section isn't going to Dallas."

## Pulling Power

Carlo the property developer and his pilot buddy Pete, went bar-hopping every week together, and every week Carlo would go home with a woman while Pete went home alone.

One week Pete asked Carlo his secret to picking up women.

"Well," said Carlo "When she asks you what you do for a living, don't tell her you're a pilot – she just won't believe you. Instead, tell her you're a lawyer."

Later Pete is chatting with a hot woman when she asks him what he does for a living.

"I'm a lawyer," says Pete.

The woman smiles and asks, "Want to go back to my place? It's only five minutes' walk away."

They go to her place, have some fun and an hour or so later, Pete is back in the pub telling Carlo about his success.

"I've only been a lawyer for an hour," Pete snickered, "And I've already screwed someone."

## Train Passengers

A pilot, a lawyer, a beautiful lady, and an old woman were on a train, sitting 2x2 facing each other.

The train went into a tunnel and when the carriage went completely dark, a loud "smack" was heard.

When the train came out of the tunnel back into the light the lawyer had a red hand print where he had had been slapped on the face.

The old lady thought, "That lawyer must have groped the young lady in the dark and she slapped him."

The hottie thought, "That lawyer must have tried to grope me, got the old lady by mistake, and she slapped him."

The lawyer thought, "That pilot must have groped the hottie, she thought it was me, and slapped me."

The pilot just sat there thinking, "I can't wait for another tunnel so I can slap that lawyer again."

## Extra Flaps

The pilot and co-pilot are getting ready to land. The pilot says, "I've heard this airport runway is pretty short so I may call for some extra flaps. The co-pilot acknowledges.

They break through the clouds and see the runway. The pilot says to the co-pilot, "That's a pretty short runway. Give me quarter flaps. The co-pilot adds quarter flaps.

They get closer. The pilot says, "Damn, this runway's is pretty short. Give me half flaps. The co-pilot, looking a bit nervous gives him half flaps.

The pilot now is getting pretty nervous, "Yikes, that's a short runway, give me three quarter flap." The co-pilot, starting to sweat, gives him three quarter flaps.

They're about to touch down. The pilot yells, "Holy smoke, this is a short runway. Give me full flaps." The co-pilot, panicking, gives him full flaps.

They touch down, apply full brakes and reversers and somehow manage to stop the plane.

After they come to a halt, the pilot wipes his brow and says, "Crikey - that was the shortest runway I've ever landed on."

The co-pilot looks around and says, "Yeah, but it sure is very wide."

## Pilots Reunion

A group of pilots, all aged 40, discussed where they should meet for lunch. They agreed they would meet at a place called The White Horse because the place had a great atmosphere.

Ten years later, aged 50, the pilots once again discussed where they should meet for lunch.

It was agreed that they would meet at The White Horse because the food and service was good and there was an excellent selection of drinks.

Ten years later, aged 60, the friends again discussed where they should meet for lunch.

It was agreed that they would meet at The White Horse because there were plenty of parking spaces, they could dine in peace and quiet, and it was good value for money.

Ten years later, aged 70, the friends now all retired discussed where they should meet for lunch.

It was agreed that they would meet at The White Horse because the restaurant was wheelchair accessible and had a toilet for the disabled.

Ten years later, at age 80, the retired pilots, discussed where they should meet for lunch.

Finally it was agreed that they would meet at The White Horse because they had never been there before.

## Seat Of The Pants

A plane took off from Kennedy Airport.

After it reached a comfortable cruising altitude, the Captain made an announcement over the intercom, "Ladies and gentlemen, this is your Captain speaking. Welcome to Flight Number 27, nonstop from New York to Los Angeles. The weather ahead is good and, therefore, we should have a smooth and uneventful flight. Now sit back and relax... OH, MY GOD!"

Silence followed, and after a few minutes, the Captain came back on the intercom and said, "Ladies and Gentlemen, I am so sorry if I scared you earlier. While I was talking to you, the Flight Attendant accidentally spilled a cup of hot coffee in my lap. You should see the front of my pants."

A passenger in coach yelled, "That's nothing. You should see the back of mine."

## Three Daughters

A pilot was talking to two of his friends about their teenage daughters.

The first friend says, "I was cleaning my daughter's room the other day and I found an empty bottle of wine. I didn't even know she drank."

The second friend says, "That's nothing. I was cleaning my daughter's room the other day and I found a pack of cigarettes. I didn't even know she smoked."

The pilot says, "That's nothing. I was cleaning my daughter's room the other day and I found a pack of condoms. I didn't even know she had a penis."

# Chapter 8: Maintenance Issues

*Here is a list of problems reported by pilots for the maintenance engineers to fix followed by the notes the mechanics left.*

---

Pilot: Left inside main tire almost needs replacement.

Maintenance: Almost replaced left inside main tire.

---

Pilot: Something loose in cabin.

Maintenance: Something tightened in cabin.

---

Pilot: Evidence of leak on right main landing gear.

Maintenance: Evidence removed.

---

Pilot: DME volume unbelievably loud.

Maintenance: DME volume set to more believable level.

---

Pilot: Test flight OK, except auto-land very rough.

Maintenance: Auto-land not installed on this aircraft.

---

Pilot: Dead bugs on windshield.

Maintenance: Live bugs on back-order.

---

Pilot: Autopilot in altitude-hold mode produces a 200 feet per minute descent.

Maintenance: Cannot reproduce problem on ground.

---

Pilot:  #2 Propeller seeping prop fluid.

Maintenance:  #2 Propeller seepage normal – #1, #3 and #4 propellers lack normal seepage.

---

Pilot: Target radar hums.

Maintenance: Reprogrammed target radar with lyrics.

---

Pilot: Mouse in cockpit.

Maintenance: Cat installed.

---

Pilot: Number 3 engine missing.

Maintenance: Engine found on right wing after brief search.

---

Pilot: Aircraft handles funny.

Maintenance: Aircraft warned to straighten up, fly right, and be serious.

---

Pilot: Friction locks cause the throttle levers to stick.

Maintenance:  That's what they're for.

---

Pilot: IFF inoperative.

Maintenance: IFF always inoperative in OFF mode.

---

Pilot: Suspected crack in windshield.

Maintenance: Suspect you're right.

---

## Chapter 9: Pilot Pick-Up Lines

I am a pilot – I can take you into the clouds.

---

In life you are either a passenger or a pilot, it's your choice.

---

I know how to push all the right buttons.

---

Permission to land next to you?

---

I didn't know angels can be found at this altitude.

---

I'll let you pull my stick.

---

Is your runway ready for landing?

---

Coffee, tea or me?

---

Damn, you just look plane sexy.

---

Excuse me, I think you've hijacked my heart.

---

Girl, you make me lose control and I'm crashing down on you hard.

---

## Chapter 10: Bumper Stickers for Pilots

Keep calm; I am a pilot.

---

Pilots keep it up longer.

---

Warning! Pilots with an attitude.

---

Born to fly - forced to work.

---

I fly therefore I am.

---

God was my co-pilot.

---

Old pilots never die. They just don't get up as quick.

---

## Summary

That's pretty well it for this book. I hope you enjoyed this collection of airline related jokes and I hope they brought a smile to your face.

I've written a few other joke books for other professions, and these are from my plumber's joke book:-

Q: Why shouldn't you play poker with a plumber?

A: *Because a good flush beats a full house every time.*

---

Q: Why couldn't the plumber get a date?

A: *Because he was a real drip.*

---

Q: Why did the plumber keep falling asleep at work?

A: *Because his job was draining.*

---

## About the Author

Chester Croker, known to his friends as Chester the Jester, has written many joke books and has twice been named Comedy Writer Of The Year by the International Jokers Guild. He has logged many hours flying over the years and when he was asked to write this pilots joke book, he simply leapt at the chance.

If you saw anything wrong, or you have a gag you would like to see included in the next version of this book, please visit the glowwormpress.com website.

If you did enjoy the book, kindly leave a review on Amazon so that other flyers can have a good laugh too.

Thanks in advance.

## Final Word

"Once you have tasted flight, you will forever walk the earth with your eyes turned skyward, for there you have been, and there you will always long to return." — Leonardo da Vinci

Made in the USA
San Bernardino, CA
21 May 2020

72078797R00061